Tropical Storm

My journey from the jungle to the unknown…

Tropical Storm

My journey from the jungle to the unknown…

by Merms

Published by Miriam Gummert
2019

Copyright © 2019 by Miriam Gummert

All rights reserved. This book or any portion thereof may not be reproduced or used in any manner whatsoever without the express written permission of the publisher except for the use of brief quotations in a book review or scholarly journal.

First Printing: 2019

ISBN 978-0-244-24305-0

Miriam Gummert
IRRI Staff House No. 16
4013 College, Laguna
Philippines

www.merms.de

Contents

I Told My Sister I'd Write Her a Poem	7
When I'm Old	9
Midnight Astronaut	10
A Boat Ride Gone Wrong	11
Grown Up Party	13
It Starts with a Splash	14
New Year's Eve	16
El Camino de Santiago	17
Surfing Sanse	18
For Pablo	19
Unconventional Muse	20
If Fish Could Scream	22
Self Preservation	23
Open Wounds	24
Keep Out	26
Musings of the Lonely	27
Winter	28
In the Jungle	29
Philippines	30
Bangladesh	31
Croatia	32
Sweden	34
Portorož	35
Paris	37
Madrid	38
Amsterdam	40

Utrecht	41
Mindanao	43
Cebu	44
LA	45
Light Pollution	46
Inspiration	47
Snip Snip	48
Not Your Manic Pixie Dream Girl	49
She	51
Tropical Storm	52
My Mistress	53
...to the Sea	54
3AM	55
His Skin Tasted of the Ocean	56
The Surfer	57
Jayce	58
Nalini	59
Anna	60
Mia	61
Louisa	62
Cio	63
Kata	64
Blue	65
The Lighthouse	66

I Told My Sister I'd Write Her a Poem

We're passengers on an unknown ship,
voyagers through life.

We cry, we laugh, through pain or pleasure,
through harmony and strife.

We're eating out of tupperwares to spare us all
the dishes.

We're throwing buttons into wells in case they
grant our wishes.

We're living in sleeping bags on the floor of
your tiny room.

We're reading secondhand books for hours and
watching flowers bloom.

We're spending the money we don't have on
things that we don't need.

We're being reckless despite ourselves and
letting our hearts bleed.

We're joking about our pain and death and all we can't control.

We're worrying for our futures, while our fears, they take their toll.

But in the end we're nothing more than a chess game's fucking pawn,

So we'll laugh and dance and try our best to keep on keeping on.

When I'm Old

When I'm old I won't remember
The nights I slept in a warm bed,
The days I was well fed.
The comforts of my daily life
Won't play back in my head.

Midnight Astronaut

If it's raining in the night
I look to find a strong street light,
And stand so I am close enough
That the drops are glowing bright.

Then I look towards the sky
And it is as though I could fly,
With the raindrops coming down
Like shining stars I'm passing by.

For playing in the rain
Can alleviate such pain.
I know no better cure
When life's driving you insane.

A Boat Ride Gone Wrong

I'll tell you a story of a boat ride gone wrong
When the waves where too high and the wind blew too strong.
We'd spent the day diving, a day filled with fun,
And on our way back we were racing the sun.

The boat hit each wave, bow first, head on, hard,
And even so we'd all let down our guard.
How many times had we done so before?
A dozen at least, but probably more.

But then things went wrong, I remember it well.
Her bow lifted up as she broke on a swell.
We'd stood up above and seen it play out,
Her captain had just said: "She'll make it, no doubt."

So quickly he ran, and so did his crew
All the while figuring out what to do.
I watched as some wood floated on by
From the hole in the hull we hoped would stay dry.

They tied up the bow with plenty of rope,

And she would be fine, or so we could hope.

But we had to change course and we had to slow down

And my parents still feared that we all might drown.

There was no land in sight and the sun setting fast

When our rescue boat approached us at last.

But the waves still too big for the boat to get near

So we'd have to swim, that much was clear.

To my sister, who's brave, but afraid of the ocean

Swimming out there was a frightening notion,

Still, when I jumped first, she followed fast.

Her fears were my adventure, at last.

We all made it over without much delay,

Most of us divers, what more can I say?

And though it was dark then, and wet, and cold

We'd all gained a story we'll still tell when we're old.

Grown Up Party

Up upon the monkey bars
Underneath the clouds and stars
Hanging, climbing, having fun
Adult worries made undone

It Starts with a Splash

I can't see past all the bubbles
Then my head breaks the surface
Remember to steer clear of others
I look down
It's dark
Endlessly blue
The unknown
It's scary
No
Exiting
Both maybe
We're engulfed
Far below
The ground starts to form
A blanket
Ever changing
With movement
Life
So many colours
Mixing
Blending
Dancing

It's pleasant
But not quite comfortable
Never comfortable
We reach a wall
Follow it down
Never going too far
For fear of being

The great wide open
Tempts
Beckons us
To explore
The unknown
Expose the mystery
It would be so easy to sink
Allow it to swallow us
Whole
But we stay
Diligent
Observers
Never more
Evermore
And then our time is up
Soon
Too Soon

New Year's Eve

We buried ourselves, to our chests, in the sand

Too close to the fireworks, much closer than planned.

So when the light started to bang up above

My friend pushed me backwards with a violent shove.

We trembled, and gaped, and we stared up in awe.

None of the adults could see what we saw,

For they had stayed back, kept their distance, quite right.

They'd played it safe, but we owned the night.

El Camino de Santiago

Ever stretching roads ahead,
Feet no longer made of lead,

Never ending one step more.
Will it be a bed or floor?

Everyday the same routine,
Still no day twice have we thus seen.

Time slowed down since it began
Yet still too quick through fingers ran.

Now the end approaches fast
And we pray that it might last.

The friends we made, the pain we share
To nothing else will it compare,

For nothing I know holds as well
As a metal formed in hell.

Surfing Sanse

We walked with bare feet
On the cold city street
And I thought to myself:
This is living

For Pablo

There's more to life than working hard
Or money on a debit card.

Please don't forget to have some fun
And laugh too hard and get some sun,

Then take some time to have a cry
Or sit around and wonder why.

'Coz life is short, you never know
How it might end, how things will go.

So don't be scared to run and play,
And save work for some other day.

(Should it backfire, what I wrote,
Be welcome on my subpar boat.)

Unconventional Muse

I asked if I could paint you.
I recall it made you blush.
Before you meant a lot to me,
When you were still some crush.

Since then you got an upgrade.
The crush then had an end.
Your new place more important.
Your new place as my friend.

And as my friend you showed me
The things that I'd forgot
The things we do for our world
The things that we do not.

I used to be quite good at that
I never used to rest.
But then in came: the darkness
That hollowed out my chest.

But when the dark was growing,
You handed me a light.
The light was a reminder
To always do what's right.

So even when I'm hollow,
I know I have a cause
A cause to help our friends
With wings or fins or paws.

And I'd still like to paint you
And use you for my art
For you're the radiant beauty
That gave me back my heart.

If Fish Could Scream

It breaks my heart when I look at the sea
And a plastic bottle stares back at me.
And not too far off is a white plastic bag
And some fishing line waiting for a turtle to snag.

A dolphin out there is choking to death.
In an oil spill a gull takes its final breath.
Whales eating garbage and sharks left for dead.
When will this stop? Once the oceans run red?

Would this problem be as extreme
If corals could cry and fish could scream?

There's an easy way we can all do our part,
If we open our minds and we open our heart,
Then throw your trash in the bin, that's a good place to start.

Self Preservation

I claimed 'self preservation' but that was long done.

Attachment had formed from the day it'd begun.

Open Wounds

I laid my injured arm on his shoulders. Gently. As not to hurt myself further. As not to push him. My face stained with tears. My clothes stained with blood. Everything smelling of salt and iron and dirt. Still, he leaned his face into mine and kissed me goodbye. Then he was gone. Leaving me behind, bleeding out through the stitches and gauze.

The healing process was long and painful. Despite the painkillers. Because of the painkillers. It hurt too much to sit but it also hurt to lay. I slept. A lot. Too much maybe. But every time I was awake I wished I could sink back into unconsciousness. If only I could have slept until my wounds were closed. But that's not how it works. Movement helps you heal healthy. If you sleep, still until it's over, the bleeding will stop and new skin will form but once you wake things won't work the way they are meant to. Or so I was told.

I allowed myself one day to cry and indulge in self pity. One day. No more. And I held myself to that promise. Keeping back tears was easy enough. If only the same could be said for everything else. I couldn't wait for the day when I could walk without limping and look back on it all, glad that I was no longer stuck there. It took too long for my liking. Much too long. But once it was over I relished every step, enjoyed running, jumping, dancing.

The pain taught me to appreciate all the things I never knew I loved.

Keep Out

You're waiting in my dreams,
Both in the dead of night,
And in the light of day,
No matter how I fight,
To make you go away.

You're in my subconscious,
Hidden by the shadow
Of momentary thought,
Though never letting go.
Within my mind you squat.

You broke down my defence,
Please note the 'keep out' sign
Which you seem to ignore
Oh, leave this place of mine.
Of you, this, I implore.

Musings of the Lonely

I thought I was in love with you
Although I'm not sure why.
Perhaps it was but loneliness,
Fleeting, passing by.

Or maybe I'm still searching
For some fairytale romance.
And you, I guess, had looked the part
At first and second glance.

But that is put to rest now
The fantasy's dried out.
But if you called I'd run to you
Of that I have no doubt.

Winter

My toes are numb,
My fingers blue,
My nose dried out,
And my skin's thirsty too.

My scarf's turning white
And my hat's soaking through.
I want to go home
But I've shit to do.

So I suck it up
Though I'm cold to the bone
But you're wrong if you think
I won't whine and won't moan.

When everything is over
And my errands are done
I retreat to the warmth
'Coz snows just no fun.

In the Jungle

The weather's too hot,
And the air is too wet.
My room smells of rot,
But I never regret
Choosing this heat,
Which I love and I know,
Over cold feet
After a walk in the snow.

Philippines

Is there anything quite like the feel of the warm afternoon sun on your skin after a swim

Or the feel of a cool outdoor shower in the stark heat of noon

Is there any sound like the crickets, an orchestra accompanying the song of a ceiling fan

Or the sound of the rain in the midst of monsoon

Is there any sight like the sun setting behind the palm trees of your favourite tropical island

Or the sight of glowing oceans in the dim light of the moon

Bangladesh

She came up and smiled at me and I knew that was it,

On that day in Bangladesh I never will forget.

Never had I seen before, a girl so beautiful.

Since then no one has come close, and pro'ly never will.

She spoke no word of English, nor I of Bengali,

All I did was look at her and she looked back at me.

She sent her sister to fetch a flower from her place

But as she spoke she looked at me, smile still on her face

Too soon our time was over, it almost made me cry.

She gave me then the flower, and I her my bow tie.

Croatia

Hands rubbed red,
A swinging bed,
The same words said,
Repeating.

For we'd begun
A week of fun
And with the sun
Retreating.

Our practice ran
When dolphins began,
Out of the water,
Leaping.

And at the pier,
when night was near,
An anchor beer
Then eating.

Not too intense
To drink, and hence,
We climbed a fence
One evening.

Then we cleaned up
To 90's pop.
And though we're done
We'll never stop
Repeating.

Sweden

Wooden houses with red roof tiles,
Wooden boats and Viking smiles,
Camping grounds beside a lake,
Where the sun remains awake.

Swimming in the water, cold,
Hearing ancient stories told,
Going on a shoeless walk,
Over grass and bush and rock.

Playing where the trolls do hide,
Looking to the ocean, wide,
Sailing in the icy rain.
I hope to soon return again.

Portorož

The bus would come at midnight
So I had time to spare
For a nap along the beachside,
With salt still in my hair.

The sky above was pitch black,
With not a star in sight.
The kind of sky that tells you:
"It's going to rain tonight."

My backpack was my pillow,
And my jacket was too thin,
But still it was too easy
To let the sandman in.

An hour still until my bus
And rain came pouring down.
And so I ran for shelter
To the closest bar around.

That evening down in Portorož,
Tired, cold, and wet,
Is an evening of adventure
That I never will regret.

Paris

I wander Paris in the fall
On the search for les Amis:
A fictional group of rebels,
The friends of the ABC.

I'm not here for the Eiffel Tower,
Nor to find romance.
I want to know why Hugo
Loved this city found in France.

I'm here to understand them,
The characters he wrote.
I want to live their stories,
On their lives I wish to dote.

For they have helped me plenty,
They mean so much to me,
They pulled me out of darkness,
Victor Hugo's les Amis.

Madrid

I'm in love with a city
That's too far from the sea,
And though to leave's a pity
This city's not for me.

But oh, the art's exquisite
And architecture grant,
And on this too short visit
I let it take my hand

And show me quite a wonder
And put me in a trance.
It made me grow much fonder-
Some fairytale romance.

There's one park that's to die for
In late afternoon light.
But elsewhere's night sky shine more.
The city glows too bright.

Though that's too soon forgotten
When with the rising sun
A new day is calling and
New adventures begun.

But it is time to leave now,
Wake from this fantasy
Although I know not yet how.
This city can't love me.

Amsterdam

The grass is too green
Our laughter so loud
We're special, unique
We're part of the crowd

We drink and we smoke,
We play in the snow,
We try to forget
The things we don't know.

We cycle in the city
At day and then at night,
And when it's too dark
Our hearts, they come alight.

Utrecht

The chilly air reminds me
Of a night not long ago
When feet and hands were frozen
On the way to that one show.

The bus to take was hiding
And it took so long to find.
We shivered all together
With a rock star state of mind.

Purple lights were blinding
And the music played too loud
But the dark that held me tight
Melted with the cheering crowd.

It felt as though the singer
Reached down deep into my gut
And pulled out a part of me
That I guess I had forgot.

Then when the show was over,
And our hearts had all been signed,
We ran to catch the last train
With a rock star state of mind.

Mindanao

We found a spot down the almost dirt road,
A small hut in sight, some cozy abode,
Where the jungle sang and the water ran clear.
No doubt in my mind: There's magic here.

Cebu

You haven't a clue
The things you do,
The lives you screw:
All black and blue.
Oh dear, Cebu,
I wish I knew
To forget you.

LA

I looked out at the city
Of yoga pants and dope,
Where everything feels scripted.
My thoughts on it are: 'NOPE.'

Light Pollution

Can't sleep
I open my window
Climb out
Look up
Where are the stars?
The sky's cloudless
And yet
It's black above
City lights glow
"Beautiful"
But at what cost

Inspiration

You were a well of inspiration
I thought would never run dry.
Now I can't think of a thing to write
And you're not even the reason why.

Snip Snip

I see the mess upon the floor.
Touch my now bald head.
"I like girls with long hair."
That's what he had said.

Not Your Manic Pixie Dream Girl

I'm not your manic pixie dream girl
I'm not here to save your world,
Or make you smile with all my quirks.
That's not how this story works.

Look at me, I've got pink hair
And never seem to really care.
Wow! Really? I like classic rock?
You'd never guess. What a pleasant shock.

You've never met a girl like me
And argue when I disagree.
"I've know a lot of girls. It's true.
And none of them are quite like you."

You think I'll teach you how to love
The plants, and bugs, and stars above?
Or show you wonders still unknown,
And then you'll never be alone?

So I'm just meant to come along?
Do some dance, sing some song?
Fill your bland with all my spice?
That's much too great a sacrifice.

There's plenty of fish in this large sea
And maybe the one that's for me
Has rainbow scales that shine as well,
And quirks and fears and jokes to tell.

They'll love the stars all on their own.
We'll both seek out the great unknown.
There's so much colour in this world
To match this manic pixie girl.

She

She shines like the stars on a cloudless night sky.

She's curious like the child that can't help but ask 'why'.

She's wild like the break of a wave, white and blue.

She's strong on her own, and she doesn't need you.

Tropical Storm

The typhoon played the role of our saviour.
There's fun to be had in a storm.
Rain demands reckless behaviour.
Why stay where it's dry and it's warm?

Too long was the sun unforgiving,
And mosquitos in numbers too vast,
And school was to kill all that's living,
Then a whirlwind offered solace at last.

My Mistress

The ocean is my one true love,
But the mountains are my mistress.

...to the Sea

There's a salty tang to the humid air

Where skin never dries and shoulders stay bare.

My feet and my locks are both free of bounds

As I listen to the earth's joyful sounds:

Seagulls and waves sing the ocean's sweet song.

The sun beats down hot, the wind blows too strong.

This is my place, to the sea I belong.

3AM

The ocean around us became alight
As we bathed in bioluminescence,
And far above the stars shone bright.
The cool water grew warm in your presence.

Your kiss awoke then something in me
Those few hours away from the dawn,
And when the sun rose out of the sea
The last of my childhood was gone.

His Skin Tasted of the Ocean

His dark hair felt like a warm summer breeze.
Fingers ran through it. I begged time to freeze.

His skin, I knew, tasted of the ocean:
Of salt, and sun, and some odd emotion.

His eyes had a sparkle, a worn out cliché.
A weight in his hands, it asked me to stay.

His breath had been heavy and heartbeat fast.
I stayed in his bed willing the morning to last,

But only too soon the morning was past.

The Surfer

She looked at you and saw the sea:
Deep and wild, a mystery.

When you laughed she heard waves break
And a wind become awake.

Oh your eyes, an ocean blue.
How could she not fall for you?

Jayce

Tell me what to write about
Travel or the sea
I've covered that already
Then why not write of me?

Nalini

There's a girl I know,
A girl I adore.
She's always aglow
And never a bore.

Her mind is a well,
A wonderful thing,
In a pretty girl shell.
She makes my heart sing.

Anna

No matter my plans you had no complaint:

We bought white shirts just to smear them with paint,

The playground was ours, monsoon or stark heat,

We played in the mud and ran with bare feet,

We ate too much sugar, yet never enough,

And once in a while our play would get rough,

We stayed up well past respectable hours,

And danced in the stream of garden hose

showers.

We had so much fun on those countless days,

And though we grew old and went separate ways

I'll love you so, dear Anna, always.

Mia

I read of a man in a book once.
It's a book you may know all too well.
And that man, he reminds me of you, love.
And his best friend is me, can you tell?

They didn't have many possessions,
They weren't awfully well off.
What they did have they shared with each other,
And, my darling, is that not enough?

Louisa

We may live much too far away
But that's no cause for great dismay.

And though we barely keep in touch
I don't worry all too much.

For I know that our friendship's strong.
To each other we belong.

And, when next we reunite,
I know that it will feel just right.

Cio

The day I crashed your party
Was the best day of my life.
For where would I be
If I hadn't met thee?
In a place full of hate and of strife.

Kata

Keep on stepping through the pain
Clench your jaw and step again.
Knee is swollen, ankle sore,
Never the less you walk some more.
Cause you're a bad ass, tough as steel
But not so hard that you can't feel.

Blue

Blue is the ocean,
It's chaos and ire.
Blue is the calm
Of the sky up above.
Red may be lust,
And passion, desire,
But blue, my dear,
Is the colour of love.

The Lighthouse

Someday I'll have a lighthouse
A small one by a bay.
Somewhere far from the cities,
So crowds stay far away.

It shall have four whole storeys.
The topmost hold the light
That in many years has worked no more
To guide ships in the night.

One floor of beds a plenty,
And hammocks hanging high.
So when the night's upon us
You need not say goodbye.

And all along the rounded walls,
Of almost every room,
Books and games are stacked up high
For days of rain and gloom.

And in the tiny harbour
That lies within the bay,
There waits a little sailboat,
Waits for the faithful day
On which we want to stay no more,
On which we sail away.

www.ingramcontent.com/pod-product-compliance
Lightning Source LLC
Chambersburg PA
CBHW071414040426
42444CB00009B/2247